Andrea Mills

Andrea is an award-winning author of more than 50 children's books and family reference titles. Her books feature a broad range of subjects, from anatomy and animals to space and sport. This self-confessed bookworm gives regular talks at schools, book fairs, and specialist events—and enjoys the ingenious questions children ask in the Q&A sessions at the end! Andrea is a big fan of the animal kingdom and has loved writing this story about our furry friends.

Julia Seal

Julia knew from the age of five what she wanted to do for a living— draw pictures! After graduating with a degree in Graphic Design and Illustration, and then working in the greeting card industry, she finally moved onto her dream job, illustrating children's books. Julia brings her expertise, charm, and passion to all the books she works on, creating wonderful characters that delight young readers.

Owl
and
Otter

and the Big Yard Sale

Written by Andrea Mills

Illustrated by Julia Seal

Owl and Otter hadn't slept at all.
They were so excited because the day
of the Big Yard Sale was finally here!

Owl was going to run the cookie stand
with the help of her friends, Moose and
Bear. They had been busy making
yummy giant cookies all week.

Big Yard Sale

Otter was in charge of the lemonade
stand, helped by his buddies, Groundhog
and Woodpecker. They had been pouring
their delicious homemade lemonade
into bottles all week.

5

The cookie stand and the lemonade stand were right next to each other at the Big Yard Sale. Soon, the sale began and customers arrived. They loved the sweet treats and started to buy lots of them!

Each cookie cost one dollar. What a bargain! But when a customer asked for four cookies, Moose and Bear couldn't figure out what the customer needed to pay.

It was a lot of cookies, but how much did they cost altogether?

Luckily, Owl stepped in
to explain addition to them.

"If one cookie costs one dollar, then two
cookies will be two dollars, three cookies
will be three dollars, and four cookies
will be four dollars. Count them! 1, 2, 3, 4!
Four cookies, four dollars," she said as
she counted out the four cookies.

2

3

4

I cookie = $1

Adding was fun once they all got the hang of it.

If they got confused, wise old Owl said, "Be careful when you count, and you'll get the right amount!"

Addition wasn't so hard. All it meant was adding up numbers to reach a total.

Over at the lemonade stand, a bottle of lemonade
was priced at one dollar. What a good deal! A thirsty
customer asked for five bottles of lemonade.
Otter wiggled five webbed toes on his foot.

"Now, imagine each of my toes is a dollar. 1, 2, 3, 4, 5! That's
all the toes on my foot. Five bottles, five toes, five dollars!"
He turned to the customer and smiled, "Five dollars, please!"

Groundhog and Woodpecker thought this was a great idea! They started adding up on Otter's toes just to make sure their math was correct.

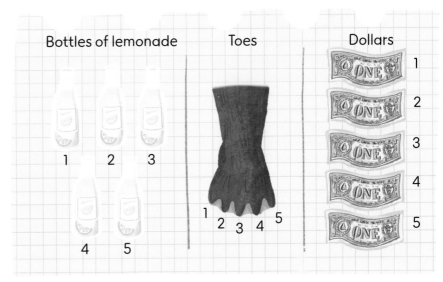

As the day went on, business was booming and eager customers were waiting to pay. Both stands were now so busy that the friends started rushing. That's when things began to go wrong.

With so many numbers to add up, the animals
got confused and mixed up their counting.

Moose even started counting backward, "5, 4, 3, 2, 1!"

"You're not launching a rocket, Moose!" Owl exclaimed.
"You're counting cookies."

Then things went from bad to worse…

As Moose and Bear squeezed past each
other to serve customers, they knocked
over two cookie jars. Crash! Bang! Wallop!
The jars tumbled to the ground and broke into
pieces. The cookies became a pile of crumbs.

Things were no better at the lemonade stand.
In his rush to sell lemonade, Woodpecker's beak
knocked against a bottle, and it fell off the
table. Smash! Lemonade poured out and
formed a puddle on the ground.

Owl and Otter realized that both stands were in trouble. There was still huge demand from hungry and thirsty customers, but the supplies of lemonade and cookies were now all over the ground.

Customers raised their eyebrows and turned away.

Owl flew over to talk to Otter, and the pair tried to figure out what to do. Moose, Bear, Woodpecker, and Groundhog waited to hear the outcome. Soon, Owl and Otter were ready to tell them.

Owl began, "The problem here is rushing to do the job. If we rush, things can end up taking longer to get done. Instead of serving customers, now we have to clean up a big mess. Let's take our time, and we'll be fine!"

They all nodded in agreement. Owl was certainly a wise old friend to have.

Otter continued, "We're still learning how to add, and it's tricky because we have so many customers. If we work as a team, we can count together. Don't panic! Count slowly—and don't forget my toes are here to help!"

He held up both feet to remind them.

1 2 3 4 5 6 7 8 9 10

They started counting out loud together, to make sure they were all doing it correctly.

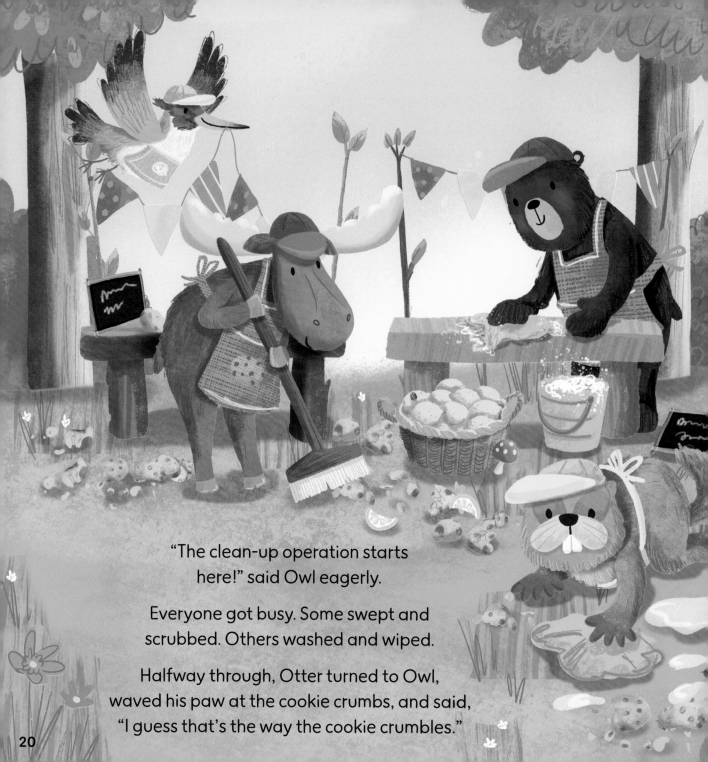

"The clean-up operation starts here!" said Owl eagerly.

Everyone got busy. Some swept and scrubbed. Others washed and wiped.

Halfway through, Otter turned to Owl, waved his paw at the cookie crumbs, and said, "I guess that's the way the cookie crumbles."

Owl nodded and waved her feathery wing at the sticky lemonade by Otter's feet, "I guess when life gives you lemons, you make lemonade!"

They burst out laughing. There was always a way to fix things and make a bad situation better.

They decided to join the two stands.

Moose and Bear used their strength to push the tables together, and make one giant stand selling lemonade and cookies. Woodpecker flew home to get more lemonade, while Owl grabbed more cookies. Groundhog put everything in neat rows for the customers.

"Great teamwork, everyone!" said Owl.

Then Otter called out, "We're back in business! Get your lemonade and cookies here!"

Lots of customers wanted lemonade and cookies.

"That's one dollar for a lemonade, and one dollar for a cookie," said Owl. "One plus one equals two. Two dollars, please."

Cookies and Lemonade this way

$1 each

+ = 2

ONE + ONE = ONE

$1 $1 $2

All the animals were enjoying adding up now! They worked hard to sell treats, do the math, and collect money.

Everything ran smoothly and easily. By helping one another and counting carefully, they earned a lot of money. They realized they couldn't have done it without one another.

At the end of the Big Yard Sale,
they collapsed into a tired heap.

Owl and Otter counted all the money they had earned.

"Wow!" said Owl. "A small fortune!"

"Unbelievable!" said Otter. "We did so well!
But what should we do with it all?"

Owl explained, "We'll open a savings account."

"What is that?" Otter asked.

"It's a special account at your local credit union or bank where money is safely stored and saved to be used later. Then you can buy something you want, like a new game, or tickets to a theme park or a show. You might also need money for an emergency."

"If we save enough," Owl continued, "maybe one day we can open a real store that sells cookies, lemonade, and other treats. Yum!"

Everyone agreed that this sounded like a very wise decision.

The friends learned so much that day,
from counting, earning, and saving money,
to running their own business!

But the most valuable thing they learned was to
help one another and work together as a team.
After all, what really counted was their friendship.

Money

Money is used to pay for goods and services. If a customer wants some of Owl's cookies or Otter's lemonade, they must use their own money to pay for it.

Addition

In math, addition is finding the total of two or more numbers. We add things together to find the total amount. Count the number of cookies on the cookie stand table...1, 2, 3, 4! The total is four cookies.

4 cookies

1 2 3 4

Piggy bank

At home, you can keep your money in a piggy bank. After counting all the money earned from the Big Yard Sale, Owl and Otter put the bills and coins in a piggy bank.

Savings account

Owl and Otter plan to deposit the money they earned at the Big Yard Sale in a savings account at their local credit union or bank. This will keep their money safe and help it grow until they are ready to use it in the future.

$AVE

Supply

Otter's team produces bottles of lemonade. The bottles of lemonade are their supply of goods, which they sell to customers. Selling their supply of lemonade to customers is how Otter's team makes money.

Demand

Owl and Otter can only sell if there are customers. The animals who pay for the cookies and lemonade create a demand for the supply of goods. The more customers there are, the greater the demand.

Teamwork

Teamwork is the process of working collaboratively with people who have different skills, to achieve a shared goal. An effective team has cooperative leaders, like Owl and Otter, and team members who help each other and work together to solve problems.

Written by Andrea Mills
Illustrated by Julia Seal

Senior Editor Dawn Sirett
Designer Rachael Hare
Senior Designer Elle Ward
US Senior Editor Shannon Beatty
Financial Literacy Consultant Allan Kunigis
Jacket Designer Rachael Hare
Publishing Assistant Rea Pikula
Production Editor Becky Fallowfield
Senior Production Controller Ena Matagic
Special Sales and Custom Publishing Executive Issy Walsh
Publisher Francesca Young
Publishing Director Sarah Larter

First American Edition, 2023
Published in the United States by DK Publishing
1745 Broadway, 20th Floor, New York, NY 10019

Copyright © 2023 Dorling Kindersley Limited
DK, a Division of Penguin Random House LLC
23 24 25 26 27 10 9 8 7 6 5 4 3 2 1
001–336386–Sep/2023

A catalog record for this book is available from the Library of Congress.
ISBN 978-0-7440-8650-8

DK books are available at special discounts when purchased in bulk
for sales promotions, premiums, fund-raising, or educational use.
For details, contact:
DK Publishing Special Markets,
1745 Broadway, 20th Floor, New York, NY 10019
SpecialSales@dk.com

Printed and bound in Canada

For the curious
www.dk.com

MIX
Paper | Supporting
responsible forestry
FSC™ C018179

This book was made with Forest
Stewardship Council™ certified
paper—one small step in DK's
commitment to a sustainable future.
For more information go to
www.dk.com/our-green-pledge